HAL LEONARD PIANO LIBRARY

SCHIRMER PERFORMANCE EDITIONS

BEETHOVEN

SIX SELECTED SONATAS
Opus 10, Nos. 1 and 2, Opus 14, Nos. 1 and 2, Opus 78, Opus 79

Edited and Recorded by Robert Taub

On the cover:
The Tree of Crows

by Caspar David Friedrich
(ca. 1822)

© The Gallery Collection/CORBIS

ISBN-13: 978-1-4234-0396-8
ISBN-10: 1-4234-0396-7

G. SCHIRMER, Inc.

DISTRIBUTED BY

HAL•LEONARD®
CORPORATION

7777 W. BLUEMOUND RD. P.O. BOX 13819 MILWAUKEE, WI 53213

www.schirmer.com
www.halleonard.com

CONTENTS

HISTORICAL NOTES

Ludwig van Beethoven (1770-1827)

THE PIANO SONATAS

In 1816, Beethoven wrote to his friend and admirer Carl Czerny: "You must forgive a composer who would rather hear his work just as he had written it, however beautifully you played it otherwise." Having lost patience with Czerny's excessive interpolations in the piano part of a performance of Beethoven's *Quintet for Piano and Winds*, Op. 16, Beethoven also addressed the envelope sarcastically to "Herr von Zerni, celebrated virtuoso." On all levels, Beethoven meant what he wrote.

As a composer who bridged the gulf between court and private patronage on one hand (the world of Bach, Handel, Haydn, and Mozart) and on the other hand earning a living based substantially on sales of printed works and/or public performances (the world of Brahms), Beethoven was one of the first composers to became almost obsessively concerned with the accuracy of his published scores. He often bemoaned the seeming unending streams of mistakes. "Fehler—fehler!—Sie sind selbst ein einziger Fehler" ("Mistakes—mistakes!—You yourselves are a unique mistake") he wrote to the august publishing firm of Breitkopf und Härtel in 1811.

It is not surprising, therefore, that toward the end of his life Beethoven twice (1822 and again in 1825) begged his publishers C.F. Peters and Schott to bring out a comprehensive complete edition of his works over which Beethoven himself would have editorial control, and would thus be able to ensure accuracy in all dimensions—notes, pedaling and fingering, expressive notations (dynamics, slurs), and articulations, and even movement headings. This never happened.

Beethoven was also obsessive about his musical sketches that he kept with him throughout his mature life. Desk sketchbooks, pocket sketchbooks: thousands of pages reveal his innermost compositional musings, his labored processes of creativity, the ideas that he abandoned, and the many others—often jumbled together—that he crafted through dint of extraordinary determination, single-minded purpose, and the inspiration of genius into works that endure all exigencies of time and place. In the autograph scores that Beethoven then sent on to publishers, further layers of the creative processes abound. But even these scores might not be the final word in a particular work; there are instances in which Beethoven made textual changes, additions, or deletions by way of letters to publishers, corrections to proofs, and/or post-publication changes to first editions.

We can appreciate the unique qualities of the Beethoven piano sonatas on many different levels. Beethoven's own relationship with these works was fundamentally different from his relationship to his works of other genres. The early sonatas served as vehicles for the young Beethoven as both composer and pianist forging his path in Vienna, the musical capital of Europe at that time. Throughout his compositional lifetime, even when he no longer performed publicly as a pianist, Beethoven used his 32 piano sonatas as crucibles for all manner of musical ideas, many of which he later re-crafted—often in a distilled or more rarefied manner—in the 16 string quartets and the nine symphonies.

The pianoforte was evolving at an enormous rate during the last years of the 18th century extending through first several decades of the 19th. As a leading pianist and musical figure of his day, Beethoven was in the vanguard of this technological development. He was not content to confine his often explosive playing to the smaller sonorous capabilities of the instruments he had on hand; similarly, his compositions demanded more from the pianofortes of the day—greater depth of sonority, more subtle levels of keyboard finesse and control, increased registral range. These sonatas themselves pushed forward further development and technical innovation from the piano manufacturers.

Motivating many of the sonatas are elements of extraordinary—even revolutionary—musical experimentation extending into domains of form, harmonic development, use of the instrument, and demands placed upon the performer, the piano, and the audience. However, the evolution of these works is not a simple straight line.

I believe that the usual chronological groupings of "early," "middle," and "late" are too superficial for Beethoven's piano sonatas. Since he composed more piano sonatas than substantial works of any other single genre (except songs) and the period of composition of the piano sonatas extends virtually throughout Beethoven's entire creative life, I prefer chronological groupings derived from more specific biographical and stylistic considerations. I delve into greater depth on this and other aspects of the Sonatas in my book *Playing the Beethoven Piano Sonatas* (Amadeus Press).

1795-1800: Sonatas Op. 2 no. 1, Op. 2 no. 2, Op. 2 no. 3, Op. 7, Op. 10 no. 1, Op. 10 no. 2, Op. 10 no. 3, Op. 13, Op. 14 no. 1, Op. 14 no. 2, Op. 22, Op. 49 no. 1, Op. 49 no. 2

1800-1802: Sonatas Op. 27 no. 1, Op. 27 no. 2, Op. 28, Op. 31 no. 1, Op. 31 no. 2, Op. 31 no. 3

1804: Sonatas Op. 53, Op. 54, Op. 57

1809: Sonatas Op. 78, Op. 79, Op. 81a

1816-1822: Sonatas Op. 90, Op. 101, Op. 106, Op. 109, Op. 110, Op. 111

From 1804 (post-Heiligenstadt) forward, there were no more multiple sonata opus numbers; each work was assigned its own opus. Beethoven no longer played in public, and his relationship with the sonatas changed subtly.

—*Robert Taub*

PERFORMANCE NOTES

For the preparation of this edition, I have consulted autograph scores, first editions, and sketchbooks whenever possible. (Complete autograph scores of only 12 of the piano sonatas—plus the autograph of only the first movement of Sonata Op.81a—have survived.) I have also read Beethoven's letters with particular attention to his many remarks concerning performances of his day and the lists of specific changes/corrections that he sent to publishers. We all know—as did Beethoven—that musical notation is imperfect, but it is the closest representation we have to the artistic ideal of a composer. We strive to represent that ideal as thoroughly and accurately as possible.

General Observations

Tempo

My recordings of these sonatas are included in the published volume. I have also included my suggestions for tempo (metronome markings) for each sonata, at the beginning of each movement.

Fingering

I have included Beethoven's own fingering suggestions. His fingerings—intended not only for himself (in earlier sonatas) but primarily for successive generations of pianists—often reveal intensely musical intentions in their shaping of musical contour and molding of the hands to create specific muical textures. I have added my own fingering suggestions, all of which are aimed at creating meaningful musical constructs. As a general guide, I believe in minimizing hand motions as much as possible, and therefore many of my fingering suggestions are based on the pianist's hands proceeding in a straight line as long as musically viable and physically practicable. I also believe that the pianist can develop senses of tactile feeling for specific musical patterns.

Pedaling

I have also included Beethoven's pedal markings in this edition. These indications are integral parts of the musical fabric. However, since most often no pedal indication is offered, whenever necessary one should use the right pedal—sparingly and subtly—to help achieve legato playing as well as to enhance sonorities.

Ornamentation

My suggestions regarding ornamental turns concern the notion of keeping the contour smooth while providing an expressive musical gesture with an increased sense of forward direction. The actual starting note of a turn depends on the specific context: if it is preceded by the same note (as in Sonata Op. 10 no. 2, second movement, m. 42), then I would suggest that the turn is four notes, starting on the upper neighbor: upper neighbor, main note, lower neighbor, main note.

Sonata in F Major, Op. 10 no. 2:
second movement, m. 42, r.h.

However, if the turn is preceded by another note (as in Sonata Op. 10 no. 2, first movement, m. 38), then the turn could be five notes in total, starting on the main note: main note, upper neighbor, main note, lower neighbor, main note.

Sonata in F Major, Op. 10 no. 2:
first movement, m. 38, r.h.

Whenever Beethoven included an afterbeat (Nachschlag) for a trill, I have included it as well. When he did not, I have not added any.

About the Edition

Footnotes within the musical score offer contextual explanations and alternatives based on earlier representations of the music (first editions, autograph scores) that Beethoven had seen and corrected. In specific cases that are visible only in the autograph score, I explain the reasons and context for my choices of musical representation. Other footnotes are intended to clarify ways of playing specific ornaments.

Above all, Beethoven's sonatas—as individual works, or taken together as a complete cycle—are pieces that we can listen to, learn, play, put away, re-learn, and perform again over and over—with only increasing joy, involvement, and meaning. For those of you looking at the musical score as you follow a recording, welcome. For those playing these pieces for the first time, I invite you to become involved. And for those returning to these sonatas after learning them previously—or comparing this edition to any other—I invite you to roll up your sleeves and start playing, for there is always more to do.

The expressive universe conjured up by the Beethoven piano sonatas is unprecedented, and unequalled.

Notes on the Sonatas*

Beethoven worked on the three Sonatas Op. 10 simultaneously beginning in 1796, completing and publishing them all by 1798. The 9 October 1799 edition of the *Allgemeine Musikalische Zeitung* includes a review of Op. 10:

> It is not to be denied that Hr. v. B. is a man of genius, possessed of originality and who goes his own way. In this he is assured by his extraordinary thoroughness in the higher style of writing and his unusual command of the instrument for which he writes, he being unquestionably one of the best pianoforte composers and players of our time. His abundance of ideas, of which a striving genius never seems to be able to let go so soon as it has got possession of a subject worthy of his fancy, only too frequently leads him to pile up ideas, etc. Fancy, in the extraordinary degree which Beethoven possesses, supported, too, by extraordinary knowledge, is a valuable possession,

and, indeed, an indispensable one for a composer, etc. The critic, who after he has tried to accustom himself more and more to Hr. Beethoven's manner, has learned to admire him more than he did at first, can scarcely suppress the wish that…it might occur to this fanciful composer to practice a certain economy in his labors… This tenth collection, as the critic has said, seems deserving of high praise. Good invention, and earnest, manly style…well-ordered thoughts in every part, difficulties not carried to an excess, an entertaining treatment of the harmony—lift these sonatas above the many.[1]

Sonata in C minor, Opus 10 no. 1 (1796–98)
First Movement: Allegro molto e con brio

After having established himself with the four-movement sonatas of Op. 2 and Op. 7, Beethoven compressed the sonata to three movments in Op. 10 nos. 1 and 2. The first of these sonatas is dramatic and concise; the *forte* beginning of Sonata Op. 10 no. 1 makes audiences sit up in their chairs. The rhetorical style—propulsive dotted rhythms, abrupt dynamic changes, and C minor setting—is intense, passionate, and stormy. Music with these characteristics has been labeled Sturm and Drang (storm and stress, the latter implying an inner impulse rather than pressure), and is often associated with a Hollywood image of Beethoven shaking his fist at the heavens. The term actually derives from a German literary movement of the 1770s and was initially applied—retrospectively—to a period of Haydn's works in the late 1760s.

The opening flourish of the Allegro molto e con brio exemplifies the unambiguous manner in which harmonies are presented, as well as spanning the compass of the treble register of the pianoforte as it then existed. The tempo can be brisk, although for metrical strength and clarity, it is important to maintain a pulse of three beats per measure rather than a pulse of one. I like to make the most of the dynamic contrasts; one *pianissimo*, two *piano*, three *forte*, and four *fortissimo* markings concentrated within only the first 32 measures reveal an intense and fiery spirit. With a concern for unity, already characteristic of Beethoven, the right hand G–E-flat from m. 1 is transformed from a propulsive dotted figure into a gentle, even rhythm at the beginning of m. 32.

*Excerpted from *Playing the Beethoven Piano Sonatas* by Robert Taub
© 2002 by Robert Taub
Published by Amadeus Press
Used by permission.

Sonata in C minor, Op. 10 no. 1:
first movement, mm. 1–8

Allegro molto e con brio

Sonata in C minor, Op. 10 no. 1:
first movement, mm. 32–36

Although the harmonic motion beginning in m. 32 is actually faster than in the first theme, the surface motion is slower, and the music flows at an ambling pace.

The long lyrical lines of the second theme contrast with the short motivic fragments of the first, but rhetorical qualities—particularly large registral spans, such as the two-and-a-half-octave leap in m. 71—are still ubiquitous. The development section is primarily *piano*, but the crescendo and decrescendo markings in mm. 125–128 ensure that the high point is the dissonant E–E-flat in m. 127, thus heightening the quiet tension here. The movement could end at the penultimate cadence (m. 281) in the coda: the home key of C minor has been reestablished; the recapitulation is complete. Therefore, I elongate the rests in that measure ever so slightly, giving the impression that the movement is indeed finished. As a result of this slight delay, the *fortissimo* final cadence becomes a surprise, consistent with the high drama throughout.

Second Movement: Adagio molto

The registral leaps and juxtapositions of dynamics of the first movement are smoothed in the florid Adagio molto. I use as singing a tone as possible, with gentle but firm pressure on the keys. The quality of sound in the *forte* areas (for example, m. 17 on) is different from the *forte* areas of the first

movement: the sound here is deeper and rounder. The music reaches an expressive apex in mm. 98–99 as the theme is abstracted into octaves in the top line with full harmonies and syncopation to support—here it is nice to expand slightly in time as well as in dynamics.

Throughout this second movement, the general harmonic motion is very slow, although within the most ornate figures the surface motion is rapid. The general form and operatic character of this movement resemble those of the Adagio of Sonata Op. 2 no. 1 more closely than does any other slow movement of a preceding sonata. Sonata Op. 2 no. 1 is also the only other minor-key sonata to date; perhaps Beethoven felt that this lyrical style of major-key slow movement—rather than the more declamatory slow movements of Sonatas Op. 2 no. 2, Op. 2 no. 3, and Op. 7, which are far more registrally confined—acted as more of a dynamic foil to the dramatic intensity of the minor-key first movements. In any case, this Adagio was the last such lyrical sonata slow movement Beethoven was to write; Sonata Op. 10 no. 2 lacks a true slow movement, and the Largo e mesto of Sonata Op. 10 no. 3 is Beethoven's first sonata slow movement in a minor key, a radical point of departure. Beethoven never returned to the style of a florid slow movement in a piano sonata.

Third Movement: Finale: Prestissimo

The Prestissimo begins in an urgent whisper, as the terse first theme develops gradually over three statements of the initial rhythmic motive, analogous to the manner of motivic development in the first theme area of the first movement. After a long fermata, the more melodic second theme of the Prestissimo also accrues over three statements of its own motivic kernel. Registral leaps and dynamic extremes (*fortissimo* to *piano*) abound. Tension builds throughout this movement as Beethoven eschews any cadence on the home key (C minor). When it is finally attained in m. 100, the music begins to feel more like and ending. Since it stays in this key for only two measures, and to heighten the surprise of the entrance of the bass A-flat in m. 102, I wait slightly after the last chord of m. 101. The restatement of the second theme in the unlikely key of D-flat major (dominant of the relative major) is quasi-improvisatory, with flexibility of pulse; here Beethoven has specified both retard and calando.

The flourish of a dominant arpeggio (briefly reminiscent of those of the first movement) leads into the coda, which concludes dramatically but softly with three descending statements of the opening motive. The concluding harmony is major, but the particular disposition of the final chord (right hand crossing over to play the low C, the dominant rather than tonic pitch as the highest note) makes the cadence seem not quite final. I do not slow down here. There is no retard, only a decrescendo; the pacing of the music remains steady, and the fermata over the eighth-rest ensures the silence necessary for the drama to resolve.

Sonata in F Major, Opus 10 no. 2 (1796–98)
First Movement: Allegro

When I start to play Sonata Op. 10 no. 2, my feelings are completely opposite to those that I have when I start its immediate predecessor: in Op. 10 no. 2 declamation gives way to questioning, stormy weightiness to gentle playfulness. Careful articulation of the 16th-note triplets (as in m. 1), separating them from the staccato quarter-note that follows—as Beethoven notated—contributes to the clarity of texture and the frolicsome nature of this figure. It also allows for a marked contrast with the longer legato arched line that follows. Since the apex of the crescendo in m. 7 is actually on the B-flat (rather than on the C, the highest note of the line), the dynamics of the phrase help leave us suspended on the dominant until the next four-bar unit brings us back, although only briefly, to the tonic key (F major). The offbeat *sforzandos* (m. 31 on) accentuate the interplay between the soprano and alto lines in a fleeting excursion into a four-part texture before leading to the second theme area. Careful grading of dynamics also adds to the rich mosaic of thematic adventures, which reach their virtuosic zenith with the crossing of hands for the right-hand trills in the bass and then the treble registers.

The development area is rhythmically motivated by 16-note triplets (first heard in m.1); a steady pulse is of the utmost importance throughout the shifting harmonies. This pulse is abandoned with the fermata in m. 117, which leaves us hanging—in registral extremes—awaiting the recapitula-tion, but as a musical joke in the "wrong" key (D major). The "correct" key (F major) is reestab-lished, but not before a tangential hint a G minor, even further afield. The pianissimo here (m. 130) is the only time this theme is so soft; the dynamic markings are significant and help infuse this area with feelings of amiable questioning.

Second Movement: Allegretto

In keeping with the light-hearted character of this work, there is no true slow movement. Instead, the middle movement of Sonata Op. 10 no. 2 is an Allegretto (minuet and trio). But it is in a minor key (F minor), songful and searching in mood. The opening of this movement—initially empty octave unisons—is the longest legato line of the sonata. I use a touch to make a sound that is as smooth, bell-like, and hollow as possible, moderating only when harmonies subtly accrue beginning in m. 5—fingers well curved, wrists flexible, light pedal leading into a deeper, weightier sensation. The appoggiaturas—*rinforzando*—(m. 23 on) are poignant but are still played *piano*.

In playing the opening of the trio, I voice the portato chords slightly to the top but still maintain the warmth of the lower register in this new D-flat major texture. Nuances of touch, phrasing, and dynamic shading are many, particularly as the line ventures higher (m. 49) and is enriched with syncopated *sforzandos* and running eighth-note counterpoint (mm. 54-55 on). Avoidance of a well-established D-flat major grounding (despite the change of key signature for the trio) and a preponderance of four-bar phrases concluding in local cadences involving minor harmonies make this section seem restless as it yearns for harmonic stability. When D-flats—as hollow octaves (m. 119)—begin to be reinterpreted as the flatted-sixth degree of F minor and thereby take on a more ominous character, the sound can be direct, very soft, but portentous. Syncopations within the counterpoint of the main theme and crescendos intensify the music of the stylized minuet when it returns. This entire movement—although an Allegretto—is neither light nor playful. The tempo needs to be spacious enough to allow for both clarity of voicing and for tension in the syncopated areas.

Third Movement: Presto

The final movement (Presto) of this sonata, however, is lithe and jaunty. Although it is much easier to slur the groups of four 16th-notes into the following eighth-note, Beethoven marked them as separated, and playing them as such gives the music more of its characteristic lift.

Sonata in F Major, Op. 10 no. 2:
third movement, mm. 1–4.

In mm. 3 and 4 play as phrased, guarding against connecting the 16th-notes to the eighth-notes that follow.

The *forte* heralding the change of key at the beginning of the development area comes as a surprise. This section of the piece has the most rapid rate of harmonic change, and clarity in voicing of the mock fugato gives the impression that the music is swirling all around us. In m. 87 on, although the only dynamic indication is *fortissimo*, the counterpoint to the theme—the running 16th-notes—can be shaped by their contour, falling in dynamic level slightly as they descend, rising level as they ascend. This concept applies to the overall shape of the thematic line as well. Since both sections of this movement are repeated and the last four measures are marked *fortissimo*, I save a little strength for the last time through, making the last cadence the most conclusive.

The two Sonatas Op. 14 were composed in 1798–99. Both are rather intimate works of three movements. Although each begins with a sonata-form Allegro, neither sonata has a true slow movement. The middle movement of Op. 14 no. 1 is an Allegretto minuet and trio, and the last is a gently paced Rondo, Allegro comodo. Sonata Op. 14 no. 2—the more playful of the pair—enchants us with a theme with three variations (Andante) as its second movement. Usually a scherzo is found as a middle movement in a large-scale sonata (such as Op. 2 no. 2), but Sonata Op. 14 no. 2 concludes with a Scherzo, Allegro assai.

Beethoven arranged Sonata Op. 14 no. 1 for string quartet, transposing it to F major. In a letter dated 13 July 1802 to his publisher Breitkopf und Härtel, Beethoven explained his reasons:

> The *unnatural mania*, now so prevalent, for transferring even *pianoforte compositions* to stringed instruments, instruments which in all respects are so utterly different from one another, should really be checked. I firmly maintain that only *Mozart* could arrange for other instruments the works he composed for the pianoforte; similarly *Haydn* also—And without wishing to force my company on those two great men, I make the statement about *my own pianoforte sonatas also*, for not only would whole passages have to be entirely omitted or altered, but some would have to—be added; and there one finds the nasty stumbling-block, to *overcome which one must either be the master himself or at least have the same skill and inventiveness*—I have arranged only one of my sonatas for string quartet, because I was so earnestly implored to do so; and I am quite convinced that nobody else could do the same thing with ease.[2]

At age 32 Beethoven was placing himself in the company of the great masters Mozart and Haydn, at least regarding musical arrangements of original works. Notwithstanding a page in the Kessler sketchbook on which the beginning of Sonata Op. 31 no. 1 is transcribed for string quartet, no other complete sonatas were arranged for other instruments. Beethoven had proven he could make such arrangements with Op. 14 no. 1, and in his mind there was no further need to repeat the feat.

In keeping with the smaller formal scope of both Sonatas Op. 14, their main themes in all movements are more registrally confined than are the themes of many preceding sonatas, particularly Op. 2 no. 2. Accordingly the Op. 14 sonatas are more immediately "singable."

Sonata in A Major, Op. 2 no. 2:
third movement, mm. 1–4

Sonata in E Major, Op. 14 no. 1:
second movement, mm. 1-8

Sonata in E Major, Opus 14 no. 1 (1798–99)

First Movement: Allegro

The lyrical qualities of Op. 14 no. 1 are apparent from the outset as the right hand plays its ascending melodic line accompanied by the pulsating left-hand chords. I like to voice these chords slightly to the top, for the right hand compresses the ascending line made by these notes (B–C-sharp–D-sharp–E) in m. 4 to conclude the first phrase. The initially simple four-bar phrase structure is extended beginning in m. 15 as the left hand rises chromatically, and the right hand increases in intensity with the crescendo to *forte* and the staccato half-note chords. I consider the staccato markings as referring to the quality of touch and sound—sharper touch, octaves almost plucked off the keys—rather than to the duration of the sound, for the fact that these are half-notes (and not eighth-notes) indicates that the sound can be held by the pedal, creating a more pointed and resonant sonority.

The phrase extension in m. 15 hints at more adventure to follow. In fact, the second theme of the Allegro starts with a simple chromatic line, initially without harmony, along any note of which a listener expects but does not receive a clarification of harmonic context. Suspense is generated, note by ascending note, each played portato and increasing in intensity. The chromaticism of the line is broken by the F-sharp

(rather than F-natural) following E in m. 24. This skip to F-sharp heightens the suspicion that we are in B major (the dominant) for this theme, a suspicion confirmed only with the cadence at the end of the phrase in m. 30.

In the development, changing fingers frequently on the top notes of the octaves can help establish the legato sound. Perhaps a very slight slowing down toward the end of the decrescendo in mm. 89–90 adds to the harmonic preparation for the return to the home key of E major, but there is no reason to take time before the surprise *forte* entrance of the recapitulation. Careful pedaling at the end of the movement will help ensure that too much sound does not accumulate, that the dynamic level remains *pianissimo*, that the movement ends gently.

Second Movement: Allegretto

The duet in octaves between the two hands at the beginning of the Allegretto establishes this movement as essentially a lyrical one, and by the direction of the note stems Beethoven has indicated that the voicing of the chords is of great importance. The crescendo in m. 62 over an empty two-octave span is a challenge. I use the pedal to ensure a blending of the two Es, and I try to make the second grow out of the sonority of the first, even though that sonority is less on the third beat than on the first. The crescendo marking guards against making the second E softer, which would otherwise naturally be the predilection, and thus helps establish the *piano* marking in the following measure to be a *piano subito*. This *piano subito* establishes an immediate contrast between the two sections—the E minor minuet and the C major trio that follows. Although the melodic lines of both are centered in the middle register of the keyboard, the minor-key minuet has a more restless feeling, for the harmonies tend to move away from the home key of E minor (tending more toward its dominant), whereas the trio is more centered upon its local main key (C major). The short coda combines the feelings—and qualities of touch—of both the minuet and the trio to conclude this songful movement.

Third Movement: Rondo: Allegro comodo

The tempo of the last movement is designated as Allegro comodo—a comfortable allegro—implying a speed that is not too fast. As the initial right-hand octaves remain in the same register as the music heard at the beginning of the sonata, the descending left-hand triplets need to be well articulated so that the changing harmonies of the right-hand octaves can be heard. The second theme (m. 21 on) begins with a solo right-hand line that is initially harmonically ambiguous, as was the second theme of the first movement. However, instead of playing with the increasing intensity of an ascending chromatic line, I play the second theme here with questioning playfulness. Seriousness of mood is reserved for the development section; the virtuosic right-hand triplets are accentuated slightly on the first of each group to hint at an implied line. The dynamics of this line—although within the general level of forte—can be shaped with the rising and falling contours of the music. With parallel treatment of the left-hand octaves, this creates the area of greatest intensity in the entire work. The lilting syncopations in the coda—more thematic abstraction—are a further element of playfulness.

Sonata in G Major, Opus 14 no. 2 (1798–99)

First Movement: Allegro

I love to play Sonata Op. 14 no. 2: the way it begins, gently creating a melody from nothing, always moving subtly forward by small harmonic changes. Even the left hand is gentle and mellifluous: no crashing chords, no full chords—in fact, no chords of any sort. This is the first of Beethoven's sonatas to begin in this way. All the previous ones have significant simultaneities at the beginning, and except for Sonata Op. 109, so do all the following ones. When in Op. 14 no. 2 a texture involving chords finally does appear (m. 26—beginning of the second theme), the feeling is of a duet in the top line, rather than chordal accompaniment. In fact, the left hand still maintains a single-line texture until m. 36. The melodic fragments that gradually accrue as the themes grow invite a sensitive and tender touch, shaped by the gently rising and falling contour of the lines. Since each of the first two melodic fragments is repeated in the right hand the question might arise about whether to play the repetition of each fragment as an echo at a softer level. Perhaps the second one could be not so much softer as more wistful, more distant in memory, particularly since the left hand plays in a higher register and the sonority is therefore somewhat thinner.

With the addition of B-flat to the thematic melody in m. 64, the beginning of the development is plaintive but still gentle. This melody is further transformed in the beginning of m. 81, when a forte octave appears for the first time, heralding the thematic line in the bass. The ten-

sion is heightened even further by the right hand's playing 16th-note triplets against the duple 16ths in the left, and by the sharp staccato 16th-notes beginning in m. 84. Whatever slight rhythmic flexibility there might have been with this line at the start of the development is now gone; the two against three, the left-hand staccato marking, the forte dynamic all imply a strict pulse.

There is a small notational difference between the start of the false recapitulation (m. 98) and the beginning of the true recapitulation (m.124)—the former has a 16th-rest following the fermata, whereas there is no rest whatsoever after the fermata for the latter. But this small difference is significant. The rest before the false return implies a breath, a lifting of the hand and foot, a fraction of a second of silence. But the lack of a rest before the true return, coupled with a sforzando marking on the leading tone C-sharp, implies that the first D of the true return simply melts out of the sonority of the C-sharp, with the second D (the same register as the C-sharp) helping to complete the resolution and the feeling of return. The longer, sustained lines at the end of the recapitulation (as at the end of the expo-sition) lead into a short coda, in which the touch of the right hand (mm. 194–195) recalls the dramatic left-hand performance of the theme in the development, before breaking off in a sudden piano (m. 196), setting up the final cadences.

Second Movement: Andante

The chordal texture of the second movement certainly makes up for any lack of simultaneities in the first. This theme and three variations are charmingly inventive; more than rhythmic, harmonic, or registral transformations of the theme, it is the accompaniment of the main line—the counterpoint—that is varied as the music unfolds. Right before the last variation, Beethoven holds us in suspense—as if we are backpedaling—as the dominant harmony is repeated for four measures (mm. 61–64). The music can seem to begin evaporating here, time suspended, the harmony static but unresolved, and the dynamic level progressively softer. Pianistic touch becomes lighter and the pulse slightly relaxed as the right-hand chords are subtly voiced to the inside chromatic descent. Time is elongated once again in the final three measures, as the pace of the theme is augmented twofold. This helps set up the final chord, but its fortissimo dynamic—a huge joke that jolts everyone out of complacency—is always a surprise.

Third Movement: Scherzo: Allegro assai

Playfulness continues in the following Scherzo. Although this movement is in triple meter, the main theme starts with three consecutive duplets, and rhythmic emphasis frequently shifts away from the downbeat. The resulting lilt lends the music a metrical unpredictability. In mm. 10 and 12, for example, I avoid any hint of an accent on the downbeat; the trajectory of the line is to the top right-hand C on the second beat. Only in m. 16 does the downbeat coincide with musical periodicity; hence the *sforzando* and fermata. By contrast the trio theme (beginning in m. 73) is firmly embedded in the triple meter, with the separate stems in the bass of the left hand (m. 77 on) forming another layer of counterpoint to the top line. But even the trio is not immune to musical joking, for the four measures of decrescendo (mm. 105–108) are an extension of the fourth consecutive eight-bar phrase, mocking and satirical in a good-natured way. The *sforzandos* in the coda make even more explicit the antics of the metrical instability of the main theme, and the *pianissimo* ending in the deep bass completes the escapade.

Sonata in F-sharp Major, Opus 78 (1809)

Although Op. 78 is a short work, its themes are concentrated and it is intense in manner, but it is also intimate and evanescent. This sonata, one of Beethoven's favorites, offers subtle glimpses into the future: the concentration on small thematic motives is characteristic of the organic, meticulously composed works of the last period, works in which every nuance is an integral part of the whole. Distinctions between melody and accompaniment begin to dissolve in Op. 78 as thematic motives of equal importance are frequently juxtaposed as counterpoint. The very nature of its closely interrelated themes demands that each be as fully characterized and realized as possible, played so as to distinguish each theme individually but nonetheless to weave them all into a carefully constructed luminescent musical fabric.

Sonata in F-sharp major Op. 78 was composed in 1809. Its immediate predecessor, Sonata Op. 57 ("Appassionata"), was completed five years earlier; extroversion gave place to intimacy. A precedent for the two-movement scheme of Op. 78 is Sonata Op. 54, both movements of which are also in the same mode (F major). But both two-movement sonatas that followed Op. 78—namely Op. 90 and Op. 111—are of a different dramatic scheme; the first movement is more turbulent and in a minor mode (E minor and C

minor respectively), and the second movement is lyrical and introspective, in a major mode (E major and C major, respectively).

Sonata Op. 78 is in the fourth of the five groups of Beethoven sonatas; three of this group (which also includes Sonatas Opp. 79 and 81a) are heterogeneous in character, and although they do not include weighty slow movements, they foreshadow in their concentrated thematic focus the late sonatas, which were to follow with Sonata Op. 90 composed some five years later.

First Movement: Adagio cantabile; Allegro ma non troppo

The themes of Sonata Op. 78 are closely related, and I try to be precise in interpreting the musical markings in order to give each theme its own character, thereby setting each into relief against the others and simultaneously creating a sense of musical unity that encompasses the entire work. For example, the opening figure of the Allegro ma non troppo is abstracted throughout the exposition, both melodically and rhythmically.

Sonata in F-sharp Major, Op. 78:
first movement, mm. 4–5

first movement, mm. 8–9

first movement, m. 20

In the development, as the same rhythmic figure forms a counterpoint to the right-hand 16th-notes, I shape the subtle dynamics of the right hand to mirror the contour of the phrase. The dynamic level falls slightly as the line does; the left-hand dynamics reflect local harmonic changes, particularly the series of dominant-tonic resolutions.

Sonata in F-sharp Major, Op. 78: second movement, opening figure (a); first movement, mm. 31–32 (b)

Sonata in F-sharp Major, Op. 78:
first movement, mm. 47–51

I shape the dynamics to reflect the contours within the phrase.

Among the most expressive markings of the first movement is Beethoven's *te-nu-te* (holding back) which he specified in m. 24 (and again in m. 83) for three left-hand chords. At this point he also added an articulation marking for the right-hand 16th-notes:

I play these three beats at an immediately slower tempo, with a sonorous left hand and articulated right hand so that the first and fourth 16th-notes of each beat receive a little extra weight. This pattern, of course, is another manifestation of the opening rhythmic cell, setting up the top C-sharps as a steady line under which harmonies evolve to the cadence in mm. 27–28 (and mm. 86–87).

Second Movement: Allegro vivace

This same dotted rhythm forms the basis for the first of the two themes of the second movement. However, the rhythmic values are doubled and the metrical position is changed so that the figure begins on the down beat. The feeling is thus completely different, much more akin to the half-cadence figure first played in mm. 31–32 in the first movement.

The opening figure (a), which is closely related to the figure from mm. 31–32 of the first movement (b) and to the dotted rhythmic figure of m. 1 of the first movement.

The incorporation of the dotted rhythm in the second movement changes the character of this figure; the second chord is played with a sharper sound, as is the eighth-note downbeat of m. 2. The entire figure, although *forte* both in mm. 31–32 of the first movement and at the beginning of the second movement, is more incisive in the latter.

Another musical motive in this movement is the grouping of 16th-notes by twos. (This motive foreshadows linear aspects of the first theme of Sonata Op. 109.) The barring of these groups by twos rather than by the more conventional four 16th-notes—and this is very clear in the autograph score—is a direct indication that Beethoven had in mind detached two-note groups (even though playing four notes in a group is sometimes easier) and that he intended the feelings of breathlessness that this treatment engenders as the second note of each group is detached from the first of the following. The left-hand line therefore should really be as legato as possible, contrasting vividly with the right-hand groups above it and creating a situation of further contrast when the two-note groups alternate between the hands (m. 22 on). Because of the *forte* dynamic and the very nature of the two-note groups, I play this area with a lot of energy. This vigor is further intensified in m. 57 on, when the pedal is employed (and the left hand is staccato), now *fortissimo*. Because of the long pedal marking, I use a sharp staccato touch in the left hand and detach the right-hand groups sharply as well, creating a very bright sound.

In keeping with the jocundity of this movement, I like to hold the fermatas in mm. 175, 176, and 177 a long time, allowing the surprise to build with each harmony. I then play the final six measures back in tempo, with the left hand as the main line. The rambunctious character of this coda comes in complete contrast to the quiet dignity of the opening Adagio cantabile of the sonata; even though this piece lasts less than 11 minutes, it creates a fully expressive universe.

Sonata in G Major, Opus 79

So crisp and vibrant is the beginning of Sonata Op. 79 that a good performance will lift the spirits of everyone in the audience, carrying them along on soaring lines that—although they may sometimes seem to double back on themselves—always move listeners forward with unflagging energy. This sonata is one of the three (including also Op. 78 and Op. 81a) that comprise the fourth of the five periods of Beethoven's piano sonatas. Although this sonata is energetic, its overall formal scope is smaller than many. Each of its three short movements is in G—the lively first and last are in G major, the songful middle one in G minor.

First Movement: Presto alla tedesca

Before actually starting the piece, I hear the first eight measures in my mind, setting the lively musical character and the quick tempo, imagining the sharp but playful *forte* staccato touch for the opening chords. The tonality is immediately defined—no feelings of ambiguity here. This is the only Beethoven sonata in which folk elements play a role. The first movement is Presto alla tedesca; the term *tedesca* alludes to a German folk dance in rapid triple meter, popular in the first decades of the 19th century. (The Alla danza tedesca of the String Quartet in B-flat major, Op. 130, is built upon an inversion of the first theme of the Presto alla tedesca of Sonata Op. 79.)

Not surprisingly, Beethoven's treatment of *tedesca* elements is highly sophisticated. The *forte* indication at the beginning of m. 8 is both unexpected and important to the drama, for it pushes forward the momentum of the phrase at a point where one would ordinarily expect the tonic cadence to conclude the phrase. The extension of the first phrase leads to a cadence on D—the dominant—that leaves us suspended. Metrical stability also dissolves as the arpeggios that follow negate feelings of three beats per bar. I play these arpeggios in the natural groupings implied (generally groups of four notes), avoiding any accents on downbeats of intermediate measures, such as mm. 13, 14, and 15 of the first group. Reestablishment of metrical stability in m. 24 provides a sense of relief, along with the cadence on A major (dominant of the dominant) as the left hand has the main line. At the end of this second theme area, there is another surprise *forte* at a cadence; we are once again propelled past the point that would ordinarily be at the end of the phrase (m. 46).

I make sure not to rush the rests on the first beats of mm. 48–49, for not only do they set up the return to the beginning of the exposition, but they also establish a sense of the metrical importance of the second beat of the measure, a feature worked out more fully in the development area with left-hand registral leaps beginning in m. 59. Throughout the development the dynamics are terraced; that is, they are either *forte* or *piano* with only two crescendos marked, one leading to the restatement of the opening theme to mark the beginning of the recapitulation. But sensitivity to key is important, and I take a little time in the transition to the *dolce* E-flat major (m. 91). The pedal markings—indicated only in *dolce* and *piano* contexts in the development section—also help set new harmonic areas into relief. For each marking I depress the pedal only slightly, which helps create a delicate veil of sonority.

Although there are no long pedal markings in any *forte* areas of the development, the *forte* to mark the beginning of the recapitulation (mm. 123–124) is indeed in pedal, and the foot is depressed to the floor. There is nothing delicate about these measures; they are high-spirited and buoyant. So is the first ending of the recapitulation; mm. 170a–171a lead a listener to expect a G cadence, so the *forte* and the G-sharp in m. 172a are both unexpected. Therefore, I wait a little longer on the quarter-rest at the beginning of m. 172a just to set up the surprises.

The main theme is in the left hand for the first time in the coda (m. 176), so when it reappears in the right hand four bars later, it seems to be a rejoinder in a dialogue. But the conversation turns increasingly jovial as *forte* appoggiaturas are introduced in m. 184. I wait very slightly before each, giving as great a sense of lift and playfulness to each as possible. In m. 191 I voice the left-hand chords subtly to the top, as this area recalls the left-hand leaps of the development section.

The actual ending of the movement—the last three measures—is unique; there are no other Beethoven sonata endings like it. The dominant harmony is that of m. 198, but there are no repeated chords at the end, no *forte* pronouncements of the tonic. I try to play the ascending arpeggio gracefully and flowing to the top by pedaling only lightly and not allowing sonority to accumulate.

Second Movement: *Andante*

The beginning of the Andante is also unusual for Beethoven. The simple melody and the gentle bass, along with a 9/8 meter, create the feeling of a Venetian gondolier's song. Although Beethoven composed in this manner only this once, Mendelssohn was to espouse the aesthetic years later in many of his *Songs Without Words*. The Andante's eighth-notes determine the tempo. I allow the pace to expand very slightly at the apex of the crescendo and decrescendo throughout the first phrase. With the change of key into E-flat major in m. 10 and the longer treble lines and running 16th-note accompaniment in the bass, it is important not to rush. But with the group of five 32nd notes in the embellishment of the line (m. 19), again I allow the tempo to expand slightly. The *sforzando* in the transition back to G minor (m. 21) is poignant, as is the portato touch in the penultimate bar. The eighth-rests in the last bar surround the final chords with silence and a ritard would be superfluous.

Third Movement: *Vivace*

A feeling of openness is immediately reestablished by the Vivace, which is back in G major. During the first time through the first phrase, the right hand is primary, but in the repeat, I bring out the left-hand line a bit more. In m. 9, though, when the hands are in unison, they are equal in voicing. The relaxed left-hand accompaniment touch of m. 18 becomes considerably more intense in m. 21, as once again the hands are in unison and the context is a strong E minor (the relative minor of the tonic G major).

I'm greatly interested in the different expressive capacities of the theme whenever it resurfaces. In m. 34, before the first recurrence of the main rondo theme, I take a little extra time and exert a bit of extra weight on the C-natural, for this helps establish the home key of G major. Here the theme is still quiet, even though the left hand is embellished with triplets which I play very evenly. But in m. 72 when the theme recurs after the longest episode, the G major tonality is established by the bass. Although the theme's right-hand notes are the same, the 16th-notes of the accompaniment provide an undercurrent of motion, making this the most intense occurrence of the theme.

The previous episode (mm. 51–71) is centered upon C major and F major; a focus upon subdominant keys rather than upon the more usual dominant helps impart a rustic character to music. Voicing in this area alternates between the hands; the left hand leads when both hands have scalar passages of 16th-notes, but the right hand takes over when the left hand plays chords.

The intensity of the thematic statement that begins in m. 72 is altered by the introduction of offbeat right-hand octave triplet eighths beginning in m. 80. Here it is important for the left hand to maintain the quarter-note pulse. I make the contrasts of following dynamics simple and stark. Over the last five measures, the crescendo begun in m. 113 continues through the first beat of m. 116, then I wait before the *piano subito*. Once again, the movement concludes in tempo—playfully but softly—with no ritard.

—*Robert Taub*

Footnotes

1. Alexander Wheelock Thayer, *Thayer's Life of Beethoven* (Princeton: Princeton University Press, 1973), 278–279.

2. Emily Anderson, *The Letters of Beethoven* (New York: St. Martin's Press; London: Macmillan, 1961), 74–75.

Dedicated to Countess Anna Margarete von Browne

Sonata in C minor

Ludwig van Beethoven
Opus 10 no. 1

Allegro molto e con brio [♩. = 76]

*As in the First Edition.

Adagio molto [♪ = 60]

* also in m. 3, 9, 11, *etc.*

****The arpeggio is played on the fourth 16th-note.

*The turn is played before the *e-flat* so that note retains its full 32nd-note value.

**The *a-flat* in the manuscript (lost) may have been tied over.

FINALE
Prestissimo [♩ = 96]

Dedicated to Countess Anna Margarete von Browne

Sonata in F Major

Ludwig van Beethoven
Opus 10 no. 2

Allegretto [♩. = 56]

*expressive short appoggiatura:

*p as in the First Edition (Eder, 1798)

Dedicated to Baroness Josefa von Braun

Sonata in E Major

Ludwig van Beethoven
Opus 14 no. 1

the turn occurs on the first 8th-note

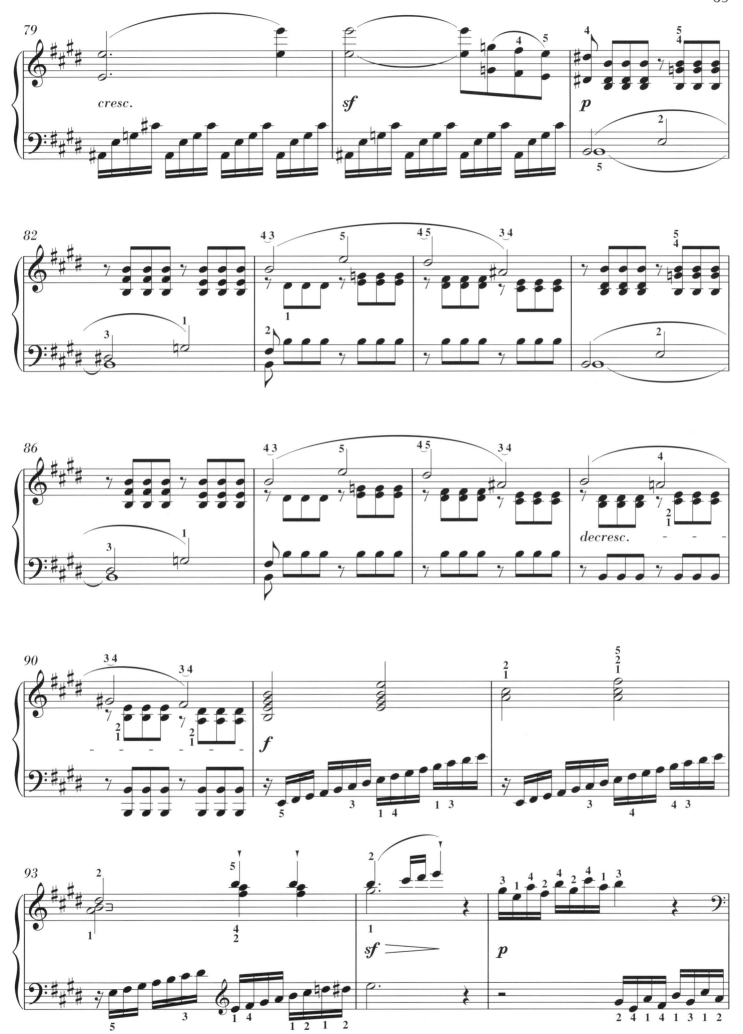

*Thus in the First Editions of Mollo and Simrock; in some recent editions, this passage is changed in accordance with mm. 44-45, a version which could not be played on Beethoven's pianos, with their more limited registral range.

Allegretto [♩. = 50]

RONDO
Allegro comodo [♩ = 80]

*Thus in the First Edition, in contrast to m. 25. The dominant harmony in m. 25 carries more weight.

Sonata in G Major

Ludwig van Beethoven
Opus 14 no. 2

*short appoggiatura
**Play the ornament before beat 1, i.e., at the end of the previous measure.

*Thus in the First Editions of Mollo and Simrock; in some recent editions, this passage is changed to be parallel to m. 170; such a synthetic version would go beyond the highest register of Beethoven's piano.

*Thus in the First Editions; in some recent editions as in m. 4: $\quad$ *cf.* footnote to m. 43 with regard to register.

Andante [♩ = 72]
La prima parte senza replica

sempre legato

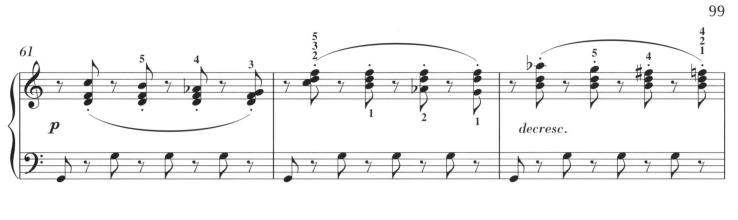

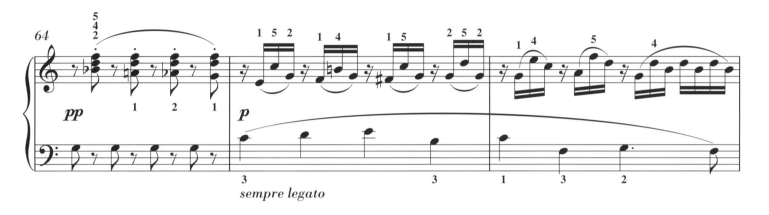

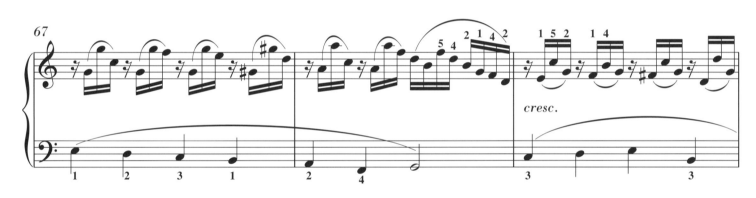

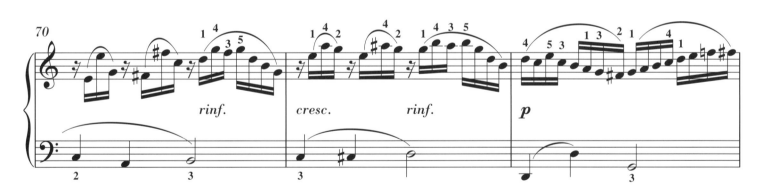

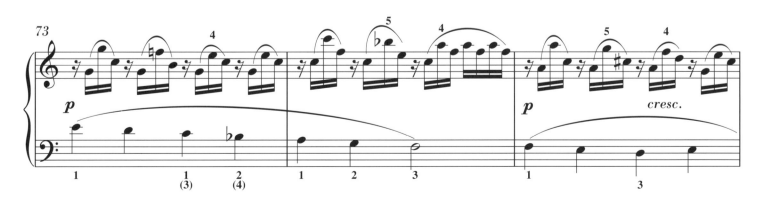

SCHERZO
Allegro assai [♩. = 72]

*short appoggiatura

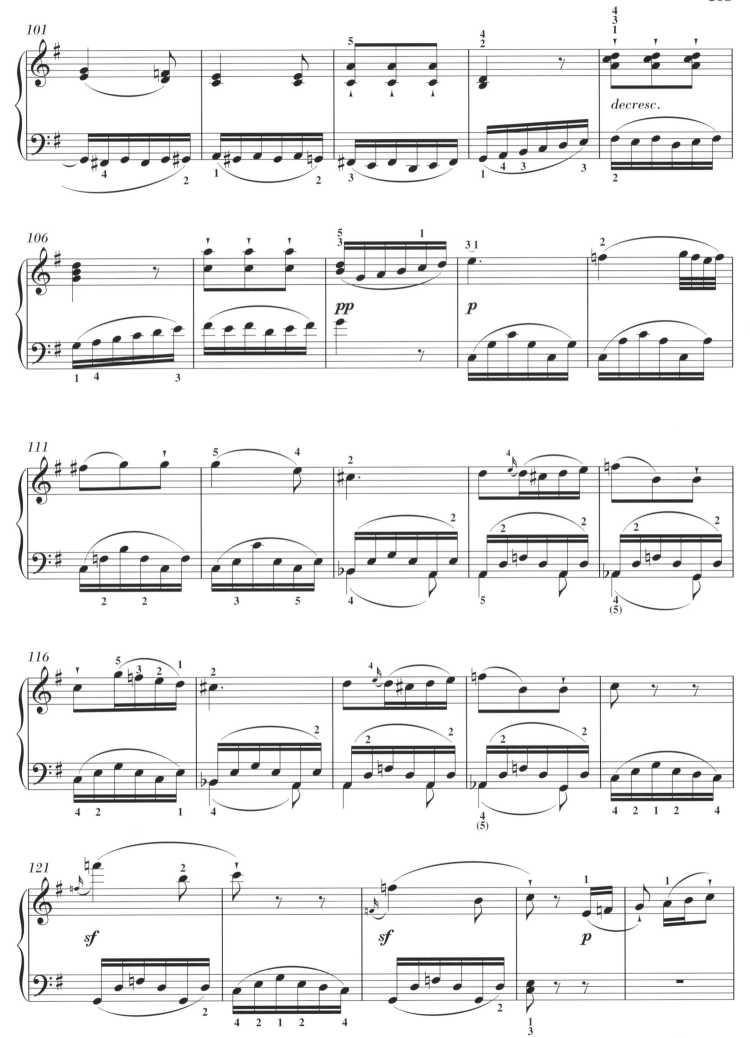

Dedicated to Countess Therese von Brunswick

Sonata in F-sharp Major

Ludwig van Beethoven
Opus 78

*The fingering in italics and the pedal markings are Beethoven's.

*In the autograph score and first edition (Breitkopf & Härtel), the *sf* appears as placed (first beat of m.17) in this edition. Several other editions place this *sf* on the 4th beat of m. 16 in order to be consistent with its placement in the recapitulation (m. 75), also as per the autograph and first edition. (See footnote for m. 75)

**

***Several other editions print the chords in this measure as in order to be consistent with the the F× in the right hand.

*See footnote for m. 16. The placement of the *sf* in m. 75 is consistent with the autograph score and first edition.

*See footnote for m. 25. The C♮ in the l.h. is consistent with the autograph score and first edition.

**$\textbf{\textit{ff}}$ here (compared to $\textbf{\textit{f}}$ in m. 26) as per the autograph.

*Addition of an F♯ on the 4th beat—as per several other editions, perhaps an attempt at consistency
 with the 2nd beat—is wrong. The autograph score is clearly notated with the F♯ - G - E (beats 2,3,4)
 as a separate voice.

Allegro vivace [♩ = 132]

*left hand over right hand

*The suspension of strict meter in this measure—which is written very broadly by Beethoven in his autograph score—continues and heightens the cadential suspense begun in the previous two measures.

Sonata in G Major

Ludwig van Beethoven
Opus 79

*The pedal markings are Beethoven's.
**Note the differences in harmonies in m. 5, 56, and 127.

*without tail (ohne Nachschlag)

*See footnote to m. 5.

**Still generally *forte* here, in contrast to *piano* in mm. 66-74; mm. 83-89 and
   mm. 90-98 offer the same dynamic contrast.

*See footnote to m. 5.

**The three notes B-A-G♯ fit within the last part of the second beat.

*without tail (ohne Nachschlag)

*A few editions, including the First Edition, have a G here instead of the B♭.
The interval of the sixth here seems more consistent with the character of this
movement thus far, reserving octaves for m. 30 onwards.

*Short appoggiatura (less than a 16th in value).

ABOUT THE EDITOR

ROBERT TAUB

From New York's Carnegie Hall to Hong Kong's Cultural Centre to Germany's *avant garde* Zentrum für Kunst und Medientechnologie, Robert Taub is acclaimed internationally. He has performed as soloist with the MET Orchestra in Carnegie Hall, the Boston Symphony Orchestra, BBC Philharmonic, The Philadelphia Orchestra, San Francisco Symphony, Los Angeles Philharmonic, Montreal Symphony, Munich Philharmonic, Orchestra of St. Luke's, Hong Kong Philharmonic, Singapore Symphony, and others.

Robert Taub has performed solo recitals on the Great Performers Series at New York's Lincoln Center and other major series worldwide. He has been featured in international festivals, including the Saratoga Festival, the Lichfield Festival in England, San Francisco's Midsummer Mozart Festival, the Geneva International Summer Festival, among others.

Following the conclusion of his highly celebrated New York series of Beethoven Piano Sonatas, Taub completed a sold-out Beethoven cycle in London at Hampton Court Palace. His recordings of the complete Beethoven Piano Sonatas have been praised throughout the world for their insight, freshness, and emotional involvement. In addition to performing, Robert Taub is an eloquent spokesman for music, giving frequent engaging and informal lectures and pre-concert talks. His book on Beethoven—*Playing the Beethoven Piano Sonatas*—has been published internationally by Amadeus Press.

Taub was featured in a recent PBS television program—*Big Ideas*—that highlighted him playing and discussing Beethoven Piano Sonatas. Filmed during his time as Artist-in-Residence at the Institute for Advanced Study, this program has been broadcast throughout the US on PBS affiliates.

Robert Taub's performances are frequently broadcast on radio networks around the world, including the NPR (Performance Today), Ireland's RTE, and Hong Kong's RTHK. He has also recorded the Sonatas of Scriabin and works of Beethoven, Schumann, Liszt, and Babbitt for Harmonia Mundi, several of which have been selected as "critic's favorites" by *Gramophone*, *Newsweek*, *The New York Times*, *The Washington Post*, *Ovation*, and *Fanfare*.

Robert Taub is involved with contemporary music as well as the established literature, premiering piano concertos by Milton Babbitt (MET Orchestra, James Levine) and Mel Powell (Los Angeles Philharmonic), and making the first recordings of the Persichetti Piano Concerto (Philadelphia Orchestra, Charles Dutoit) and Sessions Piano Concerto. He has premiered six works of Milton Babbitt (solo piano, chamber music, Second Piano Concerto). Taub has also collaborated with several 21st-century composers, including Jonathan Dawe (USA), David Bessell (UK), and Ludger Brümmer (Germany) performing their works in America and Europe.

Taub is a Phi Beta Kappa graduate of Princeton where he was a University Scholar. As a Danforth Fellow he completed his doctoral degree at The Juilliard School where he received the highest award in piano. Taub has served as Artist-in-Residence at Harvard University, at UC Davis, as well as at the Institute for Advanced Study. He has led music forums at Oxford and Cambridge Universities and The Juilliard School. Taub has also been Visiting Professor at Princeton University and at Kingston University (UK).